My Straight Jacket

Nathaniel Harris, Sr.

ISBN-13: 978-1-7328104-8-8

This book was printed in the United States of America

To order additional copies of this book contact:
LaBoo Publishing Enterprise, LLC
staff@laboopublishing.com
www.laboopublishing.com

Table of Contents

Introduction

THERE SEEMED TO BE A LOT OF SHOUTING AND SCREAMING IN THE hallway. *Clang!* There was a continuous sound of metal clashing together that was making an obnoxiously terrifying sound. *Clang!* Another sound of a metal door slamming. The keys on the uniformed officer's belt continued to taunt me as he walked up and down the corridor. *Clang!*

This time, the door that I was placed behind was slammed in my face. There were guys that were behind me in this brick room asking about me, because I was the only one wearing a flannel shirt. I heard these guys saying, "Man, I wonder what he is in for?" I was having a tough time breathing while sitting in that confined space. If you haven't figured it out by now, I was in jail.

I had been sitting in this same spot for the last three hours and the only thing that I wanted to do was to make my one phone call. As I was waiting, one inmate continued to stare at me as if he knew me. He didn't know it, but I was the wrong person to mess with. Well, in my mind I thought that since I was in jail, I was as tough as any person here.

The correctional officer shouted, "You are allowed your phone call." Anxiously, I made my way to the only open pay phone to call my mother. I knew that the moment she heard what I had done and where I was, she would be so disappointed in me. The phone rang. It was answered from the other end. The operator asked if she would accept the collect call and without questioning, she graciously accepted.

"Momma, I made a bad mistake and I'm locked up." I was having this conversation with my mother even as the phone was silent.

"What did you do?" she asked. "Now, do you see what a bad relationship will get you into? Did you listen to anything that I told you about dating?" By the tone of her voice, you could tell that Momma wanted to scream, "Didn't I tell you?"

I recalled the conversations that my mother and I had about relationships when I was little. She always told me to treat a woman as you would want to be treated. She also told me to never hit a woman. She said, "If you would never hit me, then you shouldn't hit any other female."

I thought to myself, *Was that it?* If that was the case, I would never have to worry about anything. All my life, I had heard of stories of couples fighting with each other, causing relationships to be destroyed. Who would have thought that a man could be bold enough to hit a woman, something that is so precious and fragile? The thought of being in any relationship less than what I saw on the Cosby Show was unacceptable.

Raised in church, I was confident that I could stand on the principles my parents taught me as a child. One lesson that was always relayed was to wait on God for a mate. Even the time when I rebelled from going to church, I could still hear my father's words: "Let God send you the one you need. Only He can provide the happiness you need." I just knew I was next in line for a wonderful relationship, just like the ones that I witnessed throughout my life.

Not for one moment did I believe that every relationship was picture perfect. I had seen and heard the couples that fought, swore, and abused each other at any given point. It appeared as if they were happy, would break up, get back together, and then fight some more. Some would leave each other for someone else, just to get back together again to begin the same cycle all over again.

What a waste of time!

Not me!

I would never be in a relationship like that. I just knew the person that I'd find would love me and I would love her. Sadly, I did not take heed to the warnings that my father and my mother shared with me. My mother always stated, "A hard head always makes a soft behind." Unfortunately, we don't listen to other people's warnings from the mistakes they once made in their lives. Just think—I could have avoided unnecessary drama and stress if I had just listened. Now I was sitting in that cell wondering how I could get out of this straight jacket that I placed on myself.

Jungle Love

I HAD ALWAYS HAD A GREAT DEAL OF DIFFICULTY IN FINDING A GOOD woman. I never considered myself the type of man to settle down with just anyone. You can judge me if you want to, but I never really considered settling down with just one woman. Most of the women that I had met or was introduced to may not have necessarily been what I needed, but they were what I wanted at the time. A woman had to be the perfect size, the perfect height, and have the greatest smile to get my attention. Being in love was something that I was never good at. I can honestly say that I was in love maybe twice, meaning I was in any relationships that I truly cared about.

This is how the story began...yes, the beginning of the straight jacket. There I was, sitting with a co-worker named Clarence. We were at a job site and laughing about our current and future relationships. We were having a conversation about the types of women we wanted to marry. Now, what was ironic is we were both jokingly stating that the women that we would end up marrying would have to be very bossy, mean, aggressive, and love to argue. Who would have thought that what came out of our mouths would come to pass?

I'd always had friends that called themselves hooking me up or trying to set me up on dates. One particular Friday evening, I felt motivated to call this young lady that my friends wanted to set me up with. We were having cordial conversation about just about everything, and in the midst of all of the talking, she invited herself to my house for the evening. Oh, her name was Joy, and she was on her way to my house. I wasn't expecting anything. It was kind of nice to have someone just come and hang out with me.

The Meeting

I WAS EXCITED ABOUT MEETING THIS YOUNG LADY. I HAD NO IDEA what I was getting myself into, or how this girl looked. She had a low, sassy voice, which could have meant that she was overweight. There is nothing wrong with anyone being overweight, but I just always ended up with someone taller and heavier than me. I guess this would be a good time to describe myself. I am 5'6", weighing about 175 pounds, chocolate brown, bow-legged, average build, with dark brown eyes.

About twenty minutes had passed and I hadn't heard from her. I had a crazy feeling that I had been stood up and she was not coming. At that point, I was about to call it a night. Just as I was about to lie down, the telephone rang. To my surprise it was her voice.

She explained, "I'm lost and I do not know where I am."

As I gave her directions, she became more confused. I finally replied, "Stay right where you are; I'm on my way." I figured if I didn't get her attention, my truck would. I was driving in a new Lincoln Navigator.

At the Exxon Gas Station, I was looking for Joy's light green Chevy Corsica. I flagged her down and we proceeded to my house. As we got out of our vehicles, I was not able to get a real good look at her. I did notice that she had short red hair and she had on black form-fitting pants and a beige print blouse. As she walked through the door of my house, she joked how dirty and messy my house was. She actually had the nerve to say, "I don't believe you invited me out to this trash heap. It looks like a cyclone ran through here."

As I kept talking, she said, "You probably can't keep a girl after she comes over to this disaster area."

This girl knew how to press all the wrong buttons. To get back at her for talking bad about my house, I started making fun of that "poop" green car. I told her I heard her muffler rattling from the bottom of her battle-scarred old car. Man, was I on her. It seemed so natural trying to make her feel bad. I told her, "I knew that you went past my house a few times. I followed the three quarts of oil and extra antifreeze that was leaking from that piece of trash you're driving."

I realized I had said some terrible things, but she was talking about my house, MI CASA… MY DOMAIN! By her expression, I knew she was hurt. I apologized and asked for forgiveness, offering a big hug. After we made up, we actually talked and had a decent conversation.

The time passed and before I knew it, it was 11:45 p.m. She asked if she could take a nap, or she would have to leave. Even though it seemed like a long time, she had been only there for a little over two hours. So of course, being a gentleman, I pulled out a blanket and pillow so she could rest on my living room couch. I watched her as she slept. It seemed like that was the best rest she'd had in a long while.

I now had the perfect opportunity to do what I was waiting to do. I had to see what type of frame she had. You know—how fine her body was. I lifted the covers ever so gently and as I had imagined, she had a real tight body. Oh man! She was fine!

I received a text from my friends Keith and Rufus telling me they were in the neighborhood and were going to stop over. They knocked on my door as if they were trying to wake up the entire neighborhood. I opened the door and allowed them to come in.

As they walked past my living room, they noticed someone covered up on my couch and wondered who that was. I told them that this was the young lady that I was supposed to hook up with for a while, but we never did. They laughed to each other and decided to leave to go out to the club to party. I locked the door behind them, made sure she was resting, and then I went to my room to go to sleep.

I woke up around 4:15 a.m. and went into the living room just to make sure Joy did not leave. She was still there. I kindly woke her up and invited her to rest a little better in my bedroom. She looked so drained.

As she began to drift back to sleep, I covered her up and kissed her on the forehead. I gave her a small kiss on the lips and watched her eyes open slightly. As I walked away, she grabbed my hand and asked me where I was going. She made me feel like no other woman could. She only wanted me that morning, and I only wanted to make love to her like no one had ever done before.

The Relationship

We had been dating for a while now, six months to be exact. Bit by bit, I was finding out little things about Joy that were both good and bad. I found out that she had a son from a previous relationship. We got along really well and began to develop a great relationship. We would play all types of sports and games together, and basically went everywhere and did things as a father and son would.

We were huge wrestling fans and we tried not to miss watching wrestling on television. We would practice all the moves, slamming and pinning each other to the ground. We really enjoyed having fun and being around each other.

Joy had a crazy-acting mother. Her mother did something at dinner that convinced me that she was deranged. We were at the table eating, trying to enjoy the family atmosphere, and all of a sudden, her mother began to flip out. She was yelling that the lights were flicking off and on, but no one was around the switch. She kept saying that an evil spirit was in the house, and then she placed her hands over her eyes, moving them from left to right. She began to rebuke the devil and then she began to move her hands up and down. Crazy, huh? Yes, I just figured out that I was involved with a very pretty girl with a crazy background. I thought, *Oh no, what have I gotten myself into?*

That meant if the mother was crazy, Joy was going turn out just like her mother. Little by little, Joy was introducing me to the other side of her personality. I was becoming very concerned. This newfound information was exciting but then things became tricky and complicated. I was beginning to fall for her. Her son and I were getting along, her mother acted a little weird, but Joy and I were on our way to an aggressive relationship. The forecast was changing.

There was this love-hate relationship developing. Everything was great for the first year and a half, then boom, it happened. Monday through Friday we would be all over each other intimately, but on the weekends, we could not stand one another. Although we had difficult times, I always seemed to get a good laugh out of something she did. There was one time, in particular, that we made up from an ugly argument and spent a peaceful Saturday together. I wanted to do something special so I decided to make dinner that evening.

I wanted the atmosphere to provide nothing but romance. Everything was all set up the way that I thought a woman with her beauty would enjoy. I can still hear the soft music playing. I had candles lit; I prepared a wonderful dinner. The table was set and the Sunkist soda was on ice. All I was doing was waiting for my love to arrive. As we were about to eat, she took it upon herself to blow out the candles, like we were celebrating somebody's birthday. Now, I must make a confession…I needed to seek help from a higher power, a nice cold bottle of Long Island Ice Tea. Yes, I know that was crazy, but I was convinced that I was in a relationship with someone who did not know what a romantic moment was. I am not speaking of anything sexual or freaky. I provided flowers, candles, and all that mushy stuff just for her, and wow, she did not know how to receive this moment.

As the weeks and months went on, I could see how the relationship was going to the pits. It continued to be the same thing: We'd get along, we would fight, we'd make up, we would fight, we'd have wild sex, she would leave and I would not see her for about three days. I know my neighbors hated me because every time she visited there was a nasty fight. Most of time, there was a lot of pushing, fist fighting, swearing, and of course kicking and punching walls. For the life of me, I never could understand why we were beating up and kicking the walls. Truthfully, the walls weren't the ones that I could not stand...it was that evil devil-woman, Joy. Although I am making her seem like the bad one, it takes two to act like complete fools. I also had some things to deal with.

Intimacy

SEX SEEMS TO BE A TOPIC THAT NOT ONLY SCARES BUT EXCITES everyone. Men and women have an overwhelming sense of animalism. When applied correctly, it causes one's partner to become desirous and anticipating. Intimacy is defined as a closeness shared between parties, or an intimate act. This is set in a quiet and private atmosphere that normally leads to sharing with each other sexually.

This is one area that Joy and I never had an issue with. There were some things that I had never experienced until I met this stallion of a woman. I had always been promiscuous, but there were some things that she shared with me that totally blew my mind. It was almost like she paced and coasted me right into her trap of seduction. All right men, this woman turned me out! She slow-walked me into wanting her day and night. She knew how to make her body fit mine. Situations were getting bad because I could not get enough of her. I learned things about her that made her happy and turned her on, and she could not keep herself off me either.

I remember one time when we started dating, we spent the entire day doing nothing but having amazing sex. We started early in the morning and continued until the time she left my house for the evening. The one thing I learned is when you're in lust, not necessarily in love, you don't need much rest when you want some-body like we wanted each other.

Some people just know the art of seduction. Men and women know how to manipulate by using the magic trap that lies in the area between the waist and the knees. The best thing a couple can do is learn each other's strengths and weaknesses, especially in the bed-room. One thing that I've learned is the art of having sex without physically committing the act. I learned to always have an intimate conversation, whether you're together or not. It just seemed as though we were either talking about sex or we were having sex.

I remember when a telephone call was routed to me at my desk— yes, it was Joy. We had not seen each other in a few days, so we started talking about how we missed each other. I decided to take the conversation way left. We continued to talk about how we missed each other to the point that I told her, "If you come to see me tonight, I will make it a night you will never forget. After we hung up the phone, I was so proud of myself, because I convinced her to meet me at my house after she got off work.

But the terrible thing was that I had to get through the rest of the day making sure I stayed focused on my job. I had the daunting task of keeping myself straight around my coworkers and show-ing no sign of my current condition. Needless to say, I was stuck between a rock and a hard place in my body. To sum it up, I had to suffer until I got home to meet her. Man, I wanted her so bad that I could taste her. I just had this tough assignment of walking past my coworkers while trying not to be noticed.

I made it through the day, and the task of driving home while exceptionally aroused was difficult. I just wanted to get home and wait for Joy to get there. When I arrived home, I saw her car in front of my house; I had to get myself together so she would not think sex was the only reason for her visit.

She had a key to the house… yes men, I gave her a key, and she earned it. She gave me everything that I could ever want from a woman. As I entered the door and walked past the dining room table, there was a plate of food on the table with a note that read, "Eat and get your energy because you're going to need it." When I found her, she was resting in my bed with nothing on but a towel. Oh man! I just thought to myself, *It's going to be a rough evening.* I took a shower from a hard day of work, and as I was about to wake her up, I thought about her note… I ate all of the spaghetti, toast, string beans, applesauce, and drank the orange soda.

At this point she must have heard me. She woke up, came into the dining room and kissed me on my forehead while grabbing my arm. She picked me up off my feet and threw me on the bed. This girl became a wild animal! After the CD repeated itself over and over, the candles burned low, and the whipped cream dried, it was around 10:30 that night. I got home around 5:30 that evening. We must have lost track of time. I must confess, that woman almost killed me.

I was kind of glad she left; my poor body needed a chance to heal and an opportunity to stop shaking from all the excitement. She called me when she made it home, thanking me for that evening.

Things Gone Wrong

I WOULD OFTEN ASK MYSELF WHY I GOT INVOLVED WITH STRANGE and crazy women and how I ended up in this relationship. I guess to make my point, some people believe that arguing and fighting shows that you are truly in love. I remember a friend of mine was telling me about a situation that he and his ex-girlfriend were having. He became concerned and reserved with dealing with her because she told him that he only talks to her and shows any kind of emotion when he is fussing, yelling, and fighting with her. Interesting, huh? I guess to tell the truth, that is complete insanity! In my mind, I couldn't imagine anyone staying with me if I was smacking her around. No way would I put my hands on any woman.

There was a time when Joy and I were learning to deal with each other in the good times and in the bad times. We would try to do things together, especially when we were getting along really well. I was physically attracted to her and she knew how to reach me emotionally. Not to sound whipped or anything, but she knew how to please me. Without going into too many details, she knew what I liked and how I wanted it. Now on the other hand, as much as she talked about me and how she tried joking with me at times, she couldn't keep her hands off me either. At some point, it just seemed as though we would communicate with our hands more. At first, we would hit each other on the arm. That turned into smacking each other in the face. Suddenly, it turned violent. We were fighting each other, especially when we got mad at each other.

I began to try to reason with myself as to why I wanted to be in this abusive relationship. We were trying our best not only to ruin each other's life but physically trying to destroy each other. It had gotten to the point that both of us were in a terrible trap and we didn't know how to break free from each other's grip of danger.

I can recall an instance where all madness just broke loose in the living room of my house. We were planning a family day. Joy, her son and I were at home enjoying a movie that we had rented earlier that day. We were watching this movie and it seemed that the only one that was really enjoying it was her son. I don't remember what was said or even what was done, but that entire evening turned sour. I learned in my safety training that the one of the things that you need to start a fire was a good spark, especially if the atmosphere was already set up right for one.

"I hate you!" she screamed. "I wish that you would just die!" She continued to scream all these mean and evil things to me right in front of her son. We began to fuss and fight throughout the entire house. By this time, her son was hysterical and was crying, begging us to stop. I didn't like to see him cry like that, especially when I was fighting his mother. As we calmed him down from crying and tried to put the house back together, I gave her a dangerous look, as if to say that we were going to finish this later.

Around 11:30 p.m. he fell asleep. I was kind of glad that he stayed up later than he usually does because I really didn't want to fight anymore that night. I had a terrible headache and I just wanted some rest. I was in my bedroom at the time, wondering if we were going to get through the night without talking, without fighting or without trying to kill each other. As I was dozing off, I noticed a whole bunch of noise and things moving in the living room area. I got up to see what was going on and to my amazement, she was packing her bags to leave.

I asked her, "Where are you going?"

She never answered me but continued to pack up her and her son's clothes.

Again, I asked a bit more sternly, "Where are you going? Do you realize that it is 12:54 a.m.? Why are you going to leave this late, plus wake up your son?" These were questions that I just had to know. I guess after all of the questions and me trying to grab her clothes from her, she decided to respond.

"I am leaving to go to my mother's house. I don't care what time it is; I am leaving your short tail. You can stay in this nasty, miserable house all by yourself," she responded.

Now that did it! It was too early in the morning for this madness, she was making a whole bunch of noise, she was going to wake her son up, plus she called me short! That did it! I grabbed her by her arm and forcefully encouraged her to leave. She was not that easy to pull on but when you are that emotional and upset, you find energy and strength from somewhere inside. I wanted her to go but at the same time, I didn't, so what that meant that as I was pushing her out, I was in the same motion suggesting that she stay.

At this point we were really struggling with each other. I turned my head for one split second to see if her son was up during all this commotion. As I was turning back to see what Joy was doing, it felt like a ton of bricks hit me in my eye. She punched me so hard in my eye and then locked me out of my house—my own house!

As I banged on the door, I began to scream at the top of my voice that if I got my hands around her neck, I was going to choke the life out of her. I truthfully had in my mind to kill her. Now at that point, I began to analyze the current position that I was in. I was sitting outside of my house with a severe headache. My eye felt like it was literally going to fall out of its socket and I was screaming my lungs out to be let inside of my own house.

Joy, on the other hand, had the opportunity to leave me outside to sleep on the ground. I thought about this. She was resting really comfortably in my bed. She was probably cooking a good dinner. You know that you always have a big appetite after a good fight. I was hungry, sleepy, irritable and miserable. At this point, I just wanted some peace and rest. I imagined me spending the night outside and sleeping, with nothing to eat for the night. I did all I could do to calm down. I tried to count sheep, I tried counting to one hundred, and I tried to think of that "happy place."

After twenty-five minutes of beating my head against the door and trying to get her to open it, I heard the locks unlock and then I heard her running toward the bedroom. I was honestly surprised and shocked that she actually opened the door. She really must have wanted a fight tonight. So she was in my bedroom talking a lot of trash from behind a locked door. I knew that I could get past any lock and any door that was in my house, but I didn't have any-thing to use to get it open. I began to kick as hard and as much as I could until I finally got the door open. When I got in, I charged right toward Joy.

When I reached her, I used all of my pent-up emotions and punched her in her face as hard as I could. After watching her drop to the floor, I felt like a complete fool. I wanted to make things right so went to console her to make her feel that I didn't mean to hit her. As I was trying to make things better, Joy just started doing what she did the best, talking trash to me.

She said, "You hit like a big punk. That's why I'm cheating on you with someone that can make me feel like a real woman. I hate you and I'm going to find somebody to beat your tail!"

Now why did she say that? I picked her up and just began to throw her around the house like she was an old ragdoll. The entire time that I was being aggressive with her, she never raised her hands toward me. The only problem was that she continued to belittle me as a man.

The fight began in the living room, but eventually, we ended up in the bedroom closet. The more we yelled at each other, the more clothes and hangers were being thrown at each other. Somehow, someway, we ended up taking each other's clothes off. No, we weren't fighting anymore; now we were in the closet having sex. It was interesting how we transitioned from throwing each other around to throwing clothes and hangers around to ripping each other's clothes off to having sex. The thing about it was sex after an intense argument was amazing. After an hour and half of being intimate, we began to patch each other's wounds from the fight earlier. After the bed stopped shaking, we truly had no real feelings for each other. We really had nothing in common. Truthfully, we didn't like each other at all.

Did You Really Say That?

"I really hate you!"

I wanted her to hear that clearly. We were once again in the midst of one our heated arguments. She was going to start hearing how I really felt. We'd had knockdown, drag-out fights. The complicated thing was that I really liked it. It seemed like the fighting was not affecting Joy any longer.

How much pain could she take? How many times could she take being punched in the stomach and in the face? I'd kicked her everywhere imaginable. Inflicting pain had become too easy. So I came to the conclusion that fighting would not make her leave or love me anymore, so I had to devise a better plan. What could I do to really hurt her more than I had already done? I not only wanted to hurt her but to destroy her.

Now if life had an audible expletive alarm, it probably would sound after every word that I said to Joy. I had made the decision to use words to destroy her. It's funny how you begin to think about church and church quotations when you want to justify wrong. I did remember hearing a preacher say that life and death is in the power of the tongue, so my thinking was that I could talk her into taking a dirt nap. I started tasting venom every time we began to fight. This was way past being physical; this was total disgust.

21

One day, we were riding to go to get something to eat. I didn't have much to say to her especially since she had just cursed me out on the phone and then invited me to go eat. As I was driving toward Red Lobster, she had the audacity to ask me, "Do you love me?"

Maybe it was the look in my eyes that spoke how I really felt. I must have had the look of pure disgust. She was actually looking for a truthful answer. So I gave her an answer, but I was sure that she wasn't going to be prepared for it.

"Yes! I do love you! Yes! I love you! But I would love you even more if you would die right now! I wish that you would choke on your own spit! I would love to wrap my hands around your throat and just choke the very life out of you! I bit my tongue too (expletive) long! (Expletive), I hate you! I can't wait until I get home because I'm calling your best friend to come over, and I don't even care if she tells you what we're going to do. Yeah, I said it! I haven't stopped cheating on you, you (expletive)."

I felt in charge now! I basically told her things that I'd been waiting to tell her for quite a while. Was any of it true? Of course not, but it was momentarily satisfying to watch her turn beet red.

"I don't believe you said that," she screamed. I could feel it happening. The quiver in her voice was evidence that I hit a strong chord. She could have responded, but she never did. I watched her clench her fist tightly, just staring at me. I took this opportunity to pull the truck over on the beltway to embrace the fight that was sure to happen.

I wanted her to say something that sounded crazy. I made a promise that I would leave her out here on the beltway. At that point, I considered the dinner date was over! I wanted to really choke her unconscious. For all of the years of talking me down, for all of the times she cursed me out, for every fistfight, I made her feel worthless just by talking to her in a way that was not even my character.

It seemed like hours, but in actuality, only minutes had passed by as we sat in the car arguing at the top of our lungs. As we belittled each other, we didn't notice the flashing lights of the police car that pulled up behind us. The officer tapped on the driver's side window with his flashlight.

"Sir, ma'am, is everything ok?" he asked. "I rode past this vehicle sitting here four times. I wanted to do a courtesy stop to make sure there wasn't an emergency."

She began to detail every word to the officer as if he was a counselor. As he was listening to her, he kept watching me. He was using his flashlight, obviously looking for a weapon of some type. She began cursing me out in front of the officer. Man, she was letting me have it. She didn't have a thing to say while we were alone, but now that we had an audience, she was telling him everything that I said and did. Now here's where she messed up; she was about to swing at me until the officer advised her not to.

"Ma'am," he counseled her, "I did not see him hit you or even hear him swear at you. But since I've been standing here, you've done nothing but curse this poor man out, tear him apart, and then I had to warn you about hitting him. Ma'am, if anything, I can arrest you! Now I'm going to warn the both of you, if I ride through here and you're still sitting here parked, I'm going arrest the both of you!"

I don't think that he was in the patrol car before the truck was put in drive and we were heading back to the house so she could pick up her car and go back to her mother's house. Needless to say, I was still angry and I didn't get anything to eat.

Material Things

THERE WAS NOTHING THAT I LOVED MORE THAN MY LINCOLN Navigator. I spent a whole bunch of money a month between the payments, insurance and gasoline to ride nice. Every weekend, I would spend at least three hours washing and waxing my vehicle. I would go as far as going outside to wash my truck in nothing more than a pair of shorts and a pair of tennis shoes. Yes, I was trying to be cute and trying to show off what muscles I did have. I thought that this was a way to attract and meet more women, especially if Joy and I were not going to be together much longer.

And there were a few of my neighbors who thought that I was attractive. They would stop, flirt and try to get my attention. However, there were some of my neighbors who thought that I was completely out of my mind. They were looking at me, probably wanting me to go in the house and put the rest of my clothes on. I knew what it was; they were just jealous of how fine my body was or they were jealous of the fact that I was so young with an expensive truck.

When we were getting along, Joy really liked to ride in the truck with me. We looked good together, especially when we were trying to act like a family. I recall one instance when we went out to purchase some really expensive sunglasses. Even her son had a pair to wear. We really knew how to take the art of fashion to the next level. I would actually go to the mall to try to find outfits to match the color of the truck. I was showing more attention to my vehicle than anything else that mattered to me, even Joy.

For some reason when we would argue, instead of hitting on me, she would take it out on my automobile. I remember in the middle of one of our many heated arguments, instead of wanting to hurt me physically, she would begin to attack and kick dents in my truck. And it wasn't just the dents; she would spit and do every foul and unimaginable thing to my ride.

As she was abusing my truck she declared, "I'm going to treat your truck like you treat me! Just like trash!"

I didn't know what she meant until she continued to destroy what I loved so dearly, my Lincoln Navigator. I decided that fighting and hitting on her was not accomplishing anything so I decided to repay evil with evil. I now was going to destroy something of hers. I went outside to her car and kicked a hole in the rear wheel well of her car. After I did my deed, it was like she wanted to have a conversation with me.

"How do you like those apples?" I asked.

She responded, "You are nothing but a coward. You hit on women; you kick on cars; you try to destroy people's property. Why don't you pick on someone your own size?"

Pick on someone my own size? I had to remind her that she was my size and that I was only 5' in height. In the middle of this heated discussion, she grabbed her cell phone to call someone. Whoever she was talking to on the other end, they must have heard me screaming at the top of my lungs and fussing at her. She began to talk horribly about me and was disrespecting me.

I grabbed the phone and wanted to know who it was on the other end. They never responded to my demands that they reveal themselves. I told that person, "Don't worry about it; this will be the last time that you will see Joy!" After I hung the phone up, I threw it across the room, destroying the display screen and the battery case.

This relationship was heading on a crash course straight for disaster; the end was inevitable. We broke up with each other for the last time—again.

I had not talked to Joy or her son in three weeks. I just assumed that it was finally over and I could start my life over again. All right, I'll explain the way this actually went down. I really got fed up with this relationship—Joy and this fighting stuff. This was not my character at all. I began to pray to God to show me a way out of this fatal attraction. No, I wasn't super spiritual, but I did have faith, believing that God would honor and answer my prayers.

One evening, I invited a female friend over to eat dinner, watch a movie… just to keep me company. Somehow, Ms. Joy must have known that I wasn't alone and decided to call me after all this time not hearing from her.

"Hello, what are you doing?" she asked.

"Minding my business," I answered.

"Can I come over to see you?" she asked.

"This is not a good time for you to come over," I told her. "As a matter of fact, don't worry about ever coming back over here because someone else took your position and is filling my sheets!"

I do not think that she really liked what I said because an hour later, there was a knock on the door. When I opened the door, to my surprise, it was Joy. I really didn't see her or even hear her pulling up. It was like she was in stealth mode arriving at my house. She was not alone. She came with about four other girls that I'd never seen since we'd been together. All five of these hoodlums had bats, sticks and knives. They began to push on the door and were trying to fight their way inside my house. I had to use all the strength I possessed to fight off this small, crazy army.

They began to throw all types of rocks, bottles and garbage at my kitchen window. One of the bottles that Joy threw put a decent crack in the window. Now at this point I was becoming angrier by the moment. I left my house, leaped across my porch and tried to attack all of these criminals. They must have seen the rage in my eyes so they all jumped in the car to escape my wrath. When I started toward them in the car, I noticed that the car was coming toward me. At that point, I just remember hearing wheels squealing and realizing she was attempting to run me over. I gathered myself and went back to the house to make sure that my friend was fine.

I looked out the window and noticed that Joy was standing next to my Lincoln Navigator with a metal pipe in her hand. I now decided to use the law instead of fighting. As I was trying to explain to the dispatcher what was going on, it appeared that it wasn't a call of high priority.

"Ma'am, my ex-girlfriend is in my yard destroying my property," I reported.

"What does she have on? Who is with her? What is she driving? Do you have insurance?" she asked.

Now I was livid. I had an all-out war going on outside, my friend was in the living room panicking, I was on the phone with this dispatcher who was probably laughing herself silly about me and my issue. As soon as I slammed the phone down, I heard broken glass. Yes, she busted my windshield out.

"That's it!" I said. "Since the law won't help me, I'll take the law into my own hands!"

As I left the porch, I watched her driving off of my property, spinning her wheels as if she was racing in the Indy 500. She was trying to taunt me as she was driving away. Farther down the road, I noticed that she stopped her car and she and her band of miscreants started having their celebratory dance and were waving at me with the one finger salute. Man, what a mess she just made. She ruined my dinner date, she smashed my windshield, she keyed the side of my truck, she smashed the window in my kitchen and she tried to belittle me as a man. How embarrassing!

Time Away

HONESTLY, IF IT WASN'T FOR US BEING PHYSICALLY ATTRACTED TO each other, I do not believe the relationship would have gone this far. I was really trying to find a way to rid myself of this woman who was trying to ruin my life. I just needed to get this train wreck of a relationship out of my system. My desire was to have some peace and settle into a relationship with someone who would love me and want to be with me without arguing and fighting. This relationship was like working on a dead-end job. On that job, you'd put in long hours, not be appreciated, get minimal pay and there was no room for advancement.

One weekend at my home, Joy and I were just talking and trying to work through all the problems that we were having. We spent a good bit of time holding each other for once and trying to enjoy each other. The weekend would not have been normal if there weren't any type of argument or disagreement and boy, did I ask for it. It did not take Joy much time to decide to pick a fight. After all this time, I really got sick and tired of her constant cackling and arguing. I suggested that she call somebody to come and pick her up. I really didn't care who it was, as long as she was out of my house. She couldn't stay any longer. Maybe her momma could put up with her mess, but she had to go.

As many times as she'd left my house, this was the first time that she actually left without arguing, fussing or even causing a big scene. She just grabbed her overnight bag, said goodnight, and walked out of the house. Now I was getting the feeling something was wrong. She just left without any incident; she must have been up to something. My gut feeling was she was up to something crazy.

About thirty minutes had passed and she never knocked on the door to try to get back in. I looked through the window to try to find her. I decided to pretend to be worried and slipped some clothes and shoes on to see what was going on. As I was walking toward the door, I looked for my truck keys and they were missing. I looked through the entire house and my keys were gone. I opened my front door and to my surprise my truck was gone. I knew it! She grabbed my keys, took my truck and now she was gone. That's why she never made a scene, because her plan was to take my truck and go.

I ran back into the house. I called Joy's mother's house, and no one answered. I tried calling her cell phone, but it just kept ringing. I was terribly upset and was readying myself for the fight of my life. I sat down on my couch and was trying to figure this thing out. Should I call the police? Should I call one of my friends to take me into town? To tell the truth, I was mad enough to walk all the way to her mother's house.

About twenty minutes later my phone rang and Joy was laughing hysterically on the other end.

"I told you that I was going to take everything that you love away from you, she taunted.

"Where is my truck?" I demanded.

"You'll never see that truck again," she replied. "If you want the truck, come and get it!" Directly after she made that comment, she hung up the phone.

The only place that she could be was at her mother's house. I decided to call a taxicab to make my hasty journey into the city. I didn't know if the cabdriver was terrified of me, but I had to look as if I was going to kill someone. I'm guessing that the tone in my voice indicated I was serious about something. All right, I guess I should mention I had a small bat in my hand. I only brought this weapon along just in case I had to go to war with anyone that Joy might have called in as reinforcement. I was bold enough to go in town by myself, armed with just the bat and my anger. The cabdriver demanded the payment up front; in fact, I gave him forty dollars to pay for the ride.

When I arrived at her mother's house, I politely knocked on the door, looking for Joy and the location of my truck. Joy answered from a window on the third floor. After I insisted on her showing me where my truck was and threatening to kick her teeth down her throat, she threw some keys from the window, but she never told me where my truck was. I looked down and the keys were not for my truck. By this point, I'd had enough of this mess.

Since I couldn't get my hands around her neck just yet, I took my anger and frustration out on the front door. After two good kicks, the door flew open, and my aim was to get my hands around Joy's throat. I charged upstairs to the third floor to where she was to try to get my key. My intention was not to fight but to get my keys to my truck and just go home. She began the scream hysterically and yelled that I was trying to kill her. After a few minutes of this, it appeared that things were getting out of hand. I heard someone coming up the stairs to the floor that we were on. After she cursed me out of the house and spit in my face, she finally gave up my truck keys.

As I was leaving the bedroom and turning the corner leading to the steps to the second floor, I was met by Joy's grandmother, wielding a broom with a handle that was bigger than my bat. Luckily her aim was bad and her swing was slow. I was able to bob and weave to avoid getting hit in the head. I exited the house and I was now intent on finding my Lincoln Navigator that Joy stole and hid.

By the time I circled the block a few times on foot and returned to the house to find out where my truck was, there were two police squad cars parked in front of the house. Her grandmother was explaining to the officers her side of the incident.

"That crazy man has lost his mind!" she stated. "He came into the house like a raging maniac. He kicked the door in, pushed me to ground and the only way that I got him to leave was to attack him with this broom handle. He really was acting like a complete lunatic."

I tried to explain my side of the story, but obviously they didn't want to hear it. I almost got a chance to walk away with just a smack on the wrist, but I guess the bat that I had staged on the side of the house that they insisted to the city police that I harassed them with changed that. The police officers grabbed me and positioned me on the hood of the squad car and began to read me my Miranda rights. Before long, I was wearing their finest customary jewelry, which was handcuffs. I tried to plead my case to them and I even tried to persuade Joy to tell them that this was all a mistake but to no avail. I was soon in the back seat of the police cruiser heading toward the local police precinct. I guess at that point, trying to plead my case was totally out of the question.

Upon entering the precinct, I began to tremble from head to toe. I had never been in this much trouble in my life, let alone enough trouble to land me in jail. All the stories that I had heard about prison life, all of the harassment that I was told of, just seemed to pop up in my mind as I was being processed. They were processing my information and gathering my fingerprints when I heard a voice from across the hallway call out my name.

I was hoping that he wasn't calling for me. I just hoped that he was trying to get someone else's attention. As I turned around, this man walked directly to where I was sitting. At this point, I was relieved but embarrassed. The correctional officer was someone that I went to high school with. He was a musician and we played in the same band together.

He asked me, "What are you doing in here?"

I simply replied, "My own stupidity got me here. I thought that me fighting with this woman showed how much I loved her, and now look at me!"

I wasn't really sure what was supposed to be happening or where I was supposed to be going, but he began to escort me through the offices and began to introduce me to most of his co-workers. He was bringing me snacks and all types of juices to drink. He took his merry time completing the processing just to catch up on old times and to see if I was still playing in bands. The last time that I checked, I thought that you were only allowed one phone call. I must have been special because he allowed me to make several calls to get a hold of someone.

Around one o'clock in the morning he said to me, "My shift is going to be over soon. I kept you from being locked up as long as I could, but I have to put you in now, and I'm sorry! I will check on you before I leave in the morning."

Why was he apologizing? He was leaving to go home and I was staying in there until someone bailed me out. Before he unhandcuffed me and secured the door, he leaned over and said, "Please don't end up in here anymore. I don't want to see you in here again!"

Wow! I felt comforted as I was getting situated in this place. I just knew that this was the beginning of the changes that were going to be made in my life.

Records of Being Shackled

I WAS IN A CONCRETE BOX THAT THEY CALLED A HOLDING CELL. There was a concrete bench and a urinal that occupied the space. I was in there approximately forty-five minutes by myself before I was assigned any company. This gentleman was older than I was and came into the cell shaking terribly; he appeared to be more terrified than I was. I personally believe that he was weaning off some type of drug or he had been drinking.

After a few minutes, we exchanged pleasantries and warmed up to each other. We started having a decent conversation and kept each other awake for the next few hours. As the morning was wearing on us, the correctional officer that I went to high school with knocked on the window of the cell and gave me a thumbs-up signal and then he motioned me to keep my head up. Wow! I was even more encouraged despite my situation. The fact that he kept his word really made me feel good inside.

Now for the next couple of hours, they began to shuffle us around to different areas of the prison to make room for more pestilence and disturbances just like myself. While sitting in this cell, I received a revelation to examine myself. I began to look at what I had become, where I was and how ridiculous I looked sitting in a jail cell as a criminal. I guess I was trying to figure out why I had all this anger. I was asking this about a woman that really didn't care about me and was probably home laughing at me for being in here.

Our next step was to meet someone to determine our fate and then to have a video court case to determine the bail. I was in close quarters with some serious people. Everyone in the holding cell had a chance to share what they were locked up for. One person was caught robbing a store; a few people were arrested with possession of all types of drugs; I and another guy were charged with domestic violence.

After hours upon hours of hearing everyone's war crimes, it seemed as everyone was giving each other legal advice. Obviously, they had been here before because most of the people that I thought were going to spend some time in here were leaving on their own recognizance. This one inmate told me that I would be out in a few more hours and I would have nothing to worry about. There were drug dealers that were in there that were caught with large amounts of drugs on them and they were being released, but for some reason, I was still in there.

I began to get worried and fret about what was going to happen to me. Finally, around noon the next day, my case was finally reviewed by the judge. He pretty much told me the same thing that my mother used to say to me about staying away from an abusive relationship.

The judge said to me, "People die from domestic violence. I order you to have no further contact with this young lady and I am setting your bail at one thousand dollars."

Now, I got the message clearly about staying away from her and the stop fighting deal, but where was I going to get one thousand dollars from? I began to seek legal counsel from the folks that were a lot wiser than I was—my cellmates. When I was escorted back to my cell upstairs, I asked my new bunkmate what the one-thousand-dollar bail meant and if they took a check.

He explained to me that I would have to hire and pay for a bail bondsman. Once I secured someone, I would only be responsible for one hundred dollars. Man, that was the best news that I'd heard in the last few days. On the next recreation break, my plan was to call my mother and either ask her to put up the money for me or to come and get my bank card. I had one hundred dollars in my account. I had it set aside to pay a bill, but if that money would get me out of that cold place, then so be it.

As I was waiting to call my mother, I was doing all that I could to plan my escape. I was trying to get information from any of the correctional officers, but they were of no assistance. None of my law professors could help me out; it just seemed like I was out of luck. A few hours later, I called my mother, who shared the disappointing news that she could not get to my bank card.

"Baby, I cannot get to your bank card until tomorrow and I won't have any money until the end of the week. Just stay encouraged and hang in there and I will be at the office the first thing in the morning! Do you hear me, son?"

"Yes, ma'am!" I answered.

As I hung up the phone from our conversation, I was so disappointed and literally heartbroken. Things just didn't settle too well with me, so I just hung my head, covered my face and began to pray to God. Just to imagine that I would have to be confined in that place one more day made me feel dizzy and weak. I just knew that someone was listening to my prayers. I started thinking about all of the church services that I had attended when they would preach about the Apostle Paul and Silas being locked up in jail when they began to sing and pray to God. After a while of praying and singing, the cells began to open and they were freed from prison. I just knew that neither Paul nor Silas ever abused any women that were in their lives.

When I lifted up my head, there were two men in the far corner of the recreation room fighting over the use of the telephone. When I looked around the room some more, there was this older, shorter man just staring at me, trying to size me up. When I focused my eyes on him, he had this hateful look, as if to say that he was going to catch up to me and to hurt me in a bad way. Now I knew that I had to get out of that place immediately.

Twenty minutes later, the alarm sounded to signal that our break was over and that we had to return to our holding cells for the evening. As I started to get up, my name was called out for release. No one ever explained processing to me. I did not have to return to my cell, but it was a long time from the time that they called my name until the time I was released. Somehow, someone had arranged to have me bailed out of this jail. I called my mother and thanked her for the surprise of getting me out and for making this happen for me. But to my surprise, my mother did not do it. I caught a cab over to my mother's house and hugged her as if I hadn't seen her in a while. I just wanted to take a shower and sleep this experience off.

The next morning, my phone rang. Joy's mother, Sharon, called me and told me that she was the one who arranged to have me bailed out and that she knew where my truck was. As grateful as I was for what she had done, I was so upset that her daughter lied about everything and that I had spent twenty-four hours behind prison walls for a lie. I thanked her for what she had done and I began to use the rest of the day to piece my life back together. After my mom and I had breakfast and talked a little more, my mother made me promise that this would never happen again. I really had to try to make things right in my life.

An Angry Man

There was a place that I went in my mind to escape this feeling of anger. I must admit, I have an issue with dealing with pain. I'm too proud to cry or at least let somebody see me crying. Anything that anyone said to me that annoyed me, I would get upset. Joy was the only one who knew how to get me past my breaking point. I'm not sure if I was looking forward to the physical fighting or if it was the thought of her running off at the mouth.

The more she talked the more I really wanted to tune it out. I would close my eyes and imagine that I was in a room all by myself. I could hear wind blowing, chains dragging, bars slamming and then there was something else that I heard. Although I was in this room by myself with all of these other sounds, I still heard this faint, annoying sound. The more that I tried to run away, the closer this sound got to me. Wait, it's close enough now that I can hear it. I keep hearing cursing; I keep hearing things being thrown at me and I keep hearing snide remarks.

Although I thought this room was empty, it now felt like a meat locker. I became so annoyed because I kept hearing things around me but I couldn't see what or who it was. Anger! That was it! The only thing that I knew to do when I was unsure, especially when I felt threatened, was to punch my way out.

At first, there was no contact. I was punching the air. I was becoming more enraged because I wanted to shut out that sound but I couldn't. I couldn't see what direction it was coming from. My sense of sound was blocked out by my sheer desire to hurt and destroy. I was more determined than ever to hit my mark. I was being fueled by rage. It sounded like... Joy!

As I punched, I felt flesh. Like a meat locker, everything was in line. I felt every punch, I felt every blow. The more that I made contact, the better I felt. Sure, I was angry, but the pleasure of taking my anger out on something was so arousing. I felt a sense of release after every punch was thrown. I wished that it would stop and lie down, but this flesh kept fighting me back. For every punch that I threw, two more came my way. It didn't feel like a regular punch. It was stronger, more intense. The second strike was one that felt like it was designed to take me out of my misery.

That's it! I was swinging with everything within me. I didn't really know what it was that I had hold of, but whatever it was, I was going to kill it. I kept punching and kicking and punching and kicking. I felt blood all over my fist, and this excited me even more. I knew that whatever I was striking against, I could hurt. I became like an animal that thirsted for blood. I rubbed it over my arms, my head, my face, my neck. I was covered with blood.

As loud as the noise was at this point, it all came to a screeching halt, followed by a thunderous thump. Silence! I stood there shaking, wondering what I was beating on. Was this imaginary room really a meat locker? Was this somewhere real that I wanted to be? All I really knew was this room was filled with smoke. I tried to walk but I was slipping around on something wet. I wanted to see what

I was making contact with. Every step that I took, it was difficult to get my traction until... whoa!

I stumbled across something that was in obvious pain. There was a small whimper and a sound of agony. When I reached out to feel what it was, I could do nothing but drop to my knees and cry. What had I done? My anger caused me to blank out into a space where I had no regard for any kind of life. I was so excited about hurting and destroying that I lost all consciousness. I caused so much blood to spill, I caused so much hurt, and I caused so much pain!

When the smoke cleared, it was her. It was Joy. *God, I hope she is breathing. Is she breathing? Is she dead? How bad is she hurt?* The question was, did I really care?

Moving Toward Going Backwards!

THERE COMES A TIME WHEN A PERSON NEEDS HEALING FROM SOME of the things that have caused him or her discomfort and pain. Recovery is defined as returning to a normal state or regaining something that was lost. I had lost focus of who I was as a man. I was someone who respected women and cared about life itself. My assignment, at that point, was to return to that fun, loving and joyful person that I knew I was.

I made the decision to remove Joy totally from my system and to rebuild my life. I was given another chance to get this awful experience away from me and to get a new lease on life. I recovered my vehicle and traveled back to my house to make sure that everything was just like I left it. I was so relieved to be back at my own house and not listening to the sound of doors with bars slamming, keys jingling, walkie-talkies ringing and so many other people's voices. The only voice that I heard was mine! I wanted to celebrate my freedom, so I invited a female friend over to my house to just keep me company. I just wanted to start dating again. Maybe even meet someone that I could hang out with. I wanted to go to the movies, go to a nice dinner, and maybe just hang out with someone without arguing and fussing.

Months had passed and I had not heard from Joy. I didn't think that I had her out of my system; I just thought that I was delivered from evil. This had been a nice feeling. I was going out to meet new people, I was developing friendships and to sum things up, I had not raised my voice or even had my temper flare in a while.

I wanted to celebrate my birthday in a grand way. I was another year older and I just wanted to have some fun. I started my day fixing breakfast for myself and really pampering myself in the morning. I wanted to also celebrate the fact that I wasn't that angry person anymore. As the evening was approaching and as I was watching television, preparing myself for the evening, my pager began to ring. My goodness, it was Joy! She was sending me messages through my pager instead of calling me. Now we had special codes that we would use to communicate with each other. We would spell out H-E-L-L-O using numbers and then we would use other numbers to spell out messages that we wanted each other.

I received messages on my pager like *I miss you, call me, I want some* (sex, that is). Now that was the message that I was waiting on. I called her on her cell phone to see what she wanted and to tell here I was kind of happy to hear her voice. We talked for about twenty minutes and then I invited her to my house. It seemed like she was right around the corner because she arrived at my house in no time. When she came inside, we were all over each other like two wild animals, maybe even savage.

For two months, we were like the best of friends. We spent a whole bunch of time talking and not arguing; we were enjoying each other. Maybe this time we would make this relationship work, maybe there was a ray of hope to look forward to. I was thinking to myself that this was too good to be true, and why did I say that?

A week later, everything went right back to what was familiar. We just started arguing and fussing over God knows what and for no apparent reason. We never skipped a beat at all. This time, I didn't raise my hands to hit her because I was on probation and she made it a point to remind me.

She began to harass me and constantly brought up the day that I was arrested.

"You looked so stupid riding in that police car. You deserved to go to jail. How did those handcuffs feel? If you put your hands on me again, you are going right back."

Man, I thought I had gotten all of that stuff out of my system, but she knew just how to get me upset and how to twist the right screws. She started to punch on me, push me, and spit in my face. As upset and as angry as I was, I didn't have any fight in me. Every time she wanted to fight and argue, I would simply ask her to leave and to go home to her mother's house. I would beg constantly for her to stop fighting with me. I would plead for her to stay away from me, but she just wouldn't do it. I would continually ask myself why she had all of this anger. I would pray that God would guide me through this process of getting Joy out of my life, because I didn't know how to.

Around November, I was done with my probation. I checked in with my probation officer for the last time. That week, it felt like freedom to be able to do anything and to go anywhere I wanted without asking for special permission from anyone. I knew, though, that my test was going to come through that wonderful woman that was in my life. One weekend, after one of our arguments, we were at the house patching the place up and trying to act civil for a change. We were planning on spending the day together, just the two of us. We planned a wonderful evening together and we enjoyed everything about our time together.

The morning, however, was a different story. Everything was going too well, and we seemed to be laughing and playing around until she became irritating and argumentative.

"I am going to punch you in your face and there is nothing that you can do about it!" she shouted.

What she didn't know was that I was done with my probation and I was waiting for her to run her mouth again.

I said to her, "Hit me if you want to, and I'll slap the taste out of your mouth. As a matter of fact, I am going to beat the color off you, because I'm not on probation anymore, so try me!"

I do believe that was the spur that she needed. She charged at me, swinging her arms like a mad woman. My natural reaction was to do what was still inside me. The only thing that I remember was silence, a drop to the floor and then a whole bunch of crying. Yes, I had become that angry, combative person that I prayed to God that I would never become again.

We both ended up on the floor crying into each other's arms, trying to figure out what happened and what we had become over the years. We were asking each other why we kept fighting with each other and what it was going to take to stop before we either got each other into some serious trouble with the law or possibly hurt each other badly. After an hour of consoling each other, we lay across the couch and fell fast asleep.

Adult Entertainment

WE WERE FINALLY GETTING THE POINT THAT JOY AND I JUST HAD to stay away from each other. I was looking to occupy my time with something meaningful, yet entertaining. As I was out searching for my new adventure, I eventually went from one extreme to another.

I began to use my time and waste my hard-earned money frequenting the local female review clubs. I must admit, this was my new escape. I didn't want any hassles or commitments; I just wanted to be out looking at naked women. Just the thought of mostly naked women and scattered flesh in these clubs really excited me. There was one point where my friends and I would travel the entire city just to spend money on under-dressed women at the strip clubs. I loved to look at all types of women. It didn't matter what color, what type or what size; if they were looking hot, it really didn't matter. This began to be a costly habit for me, so I had to make the decision to stop before I lost everything. I had a job that took me out of the state to work. No matter where we were or what city we were in, I always took the opportunity to visit a female review club.

This was getting ridiculous. As much as I was enjoying myself, this was becoming an expensive habit. I concluded that I didn't need to spend any more money on these ladies, especially since I wasn't taking any of them home or making them my girlfriend. I was thinking about all the female friends that I had in my life and that I didn't have to do this anymore. As crazy as this may sound, I began to pray in my own special way that God would take these desires to be at these female strip clubs and to remove my desire to see all these strange, naked women.

One day, I took the day off from work and met up with my good friend Tony, and we decided to have lunch together. We decided to hang out at the Brass Kitty; needless to say, this was a strip club. We ate lunch there, but we weren't enjoying ourselves at all, so we decided to drive across town to another adult club called the Chocolate Candy Store. Now I had never been here before, but I did hear that this place was nice, they had gorgeous women, and we would have a great time there.

We got inside the club and it appeared that the party was going really well and everyone was cheering and having a great time. We wanted to get really good seats so we grabbed two stools directly in front of the stage. There was no cover charge to get inside the club, but they did require a one-drink minimum. I treated us to a Long Island Ice Tea and we were enjoying the scenery and looking to lose money. We were watching all the talent that was dancing, but we were being really choosy about who we were giving our money to. These young ladies were probably mad with us because we weren't throwing too much money to them at all. They were going around the entire club dancing really sexy, and all of the other men were giving them all really good tips. When they came over to us, they were sadly disappointed.

If you remember, I had recently prayed that I wanted to stop frequenting these adult clubs and I believed that God was about to answer my prayers. I didn't think that He would deliver me inside of the club, especially that day. To tell the truth, I enjoyed my day with my friend Tony. We ate some really good food, but I really didn't want to be here anymore. I was looking for an excuse to leave this club.

There was one female that caught my attention. I was not sure, but there was something about her that was different. Something just seemed special, but it wasn't necessarily in a good way. I was watching her as she was preparing to dance solo. As she made her approach to the stage, she seemed to be favoring her right arm. Now I knew that something was wrong. Either she was hurt from falling off the pole, possibly she slipped on the floor or… wait, she was handicapped.

No, this isn't a joke against people with disabilities or anything but this was terrible watching this person with a handicap trying to hustle money at this topless bar. Boy, I had seen it all when she began to dance or whatever she called it. She was making her way gingerly around the entire club, stopping to possibly get tips from the guys that were sitting around the bar. It was really no surprise that she wasn't receiving anything from these guys. I felt badly for her because they shrugged her off and then made fun of her as she walked away.

The wildest thing that I saw was when she was unsuccessful with the lap dances; she made her way to the metal pole that was at the side of the club. I was curious to see how this was going to play out. She grabbed her handicapped arm and adjusted it around to hold on to the pole. Needless to say, I was anxious to see her pull this off. She grabbed the arm that was wrapped around the pole with her good arm and jumped up as high as she could. She only jumped up maybe eight inches and then she began to slide herself down the pole to the floor. The funny thing was that she didn't exactly land with a perfect ten score; she actually landed really hard on her rear end.

After this act of embarrassment, I guess she wanted to make up for her poor performance by doing lap dances again. As she began, she decided to start this quest with—you guessed it—me. I really felt bad for her because of her handicap and I didn't want to embarrass her any more than she was already. I kindly told her that I didn't want a lap dance from her but I did want to give her a tip. I gave her three dollars out of the kindness of my heart—you know, just being nice and feeling badly for her. I just felt that she needed a little help financially because maybe this was the only job that she could get. If this was the case, she was going to starve to death based on what we witnessed at the club that day. We left the adult club shortly after this, and we vowed to never go to another strip club again. To this date, I haven't been to one of those flesh shops and I really do not miss anything about it.

More Evidence
to Consider

SINCE I WASN'T GETTING THE MESSAGE PLAINLY ENOUGH, I GUESS I needed proof that the relationship I was involved in was a sight to witness. I did believe that what I would witness through another relationship would prove to me that I should never allow myself or anyone else to go through this type of abuse in a relationship.

I had some friends come over to my house one Saturday afternoon. My good friends Rudy and Jarvis came over to spend some time with me. They brought along their girlfriends or whoever these young ladies were in their lives. We hadn't seen each other in some years so we spent a whole bunch of time talking about things that we used to do, especially things that we used to do at all of the dance clubs that we used to frequent. We all grew up together in the same neighborhood and we stuck together from middle school all the way through high school. As close as we were, we lost contact after we all graduated and we all went our own separate ways. Every once in a while, we would bump into each other, but this was the first time in years we had all been together at the same time.

Rudy's girlfriend, Katrina, asked him to help her out by changing their child. I saw his entire mood change from being talkative and laughing with Rudy and me to short and snappy with her. They began to fuss and curse at each other like they were a bunch of drunken sailors. This was terrible! I had not heard any of this fussing since Joy and I—I just hadn't heard this in a long time. All this was because she asked him to change the baby.

Now this is where it got really serious and scary. The yelling and the cursing were getting louder and unbearable. I just had to do something to restore the peace.

I said, "Please stop screaming at the top of your voices because my neighbors are going to call the police."

Things calmed down, but as I expected, the situation got out of hand shortly. They began to make snide comments about each other and then they began to talk under their breath, trying to provoke each other into an argument again. Jarvis, his girlfriend Angie, and I were playing referee to these two battling warriors. Katrina was sitting in the chair closest to the porch door trying to calm down; at this point, she was crying and holding her chest like she was in pain. Now Rudy was standing on the porch smoking a cigarette, trying to gather himself. It seemed like the more he smoked, the more upset he became.

He didn't make it inside the house before he did something that shocked everyone. He literally grabbed Katrina from the outside of the screen door as she was sitting.

As she stood up in front of him, he slapped her as hard as he could, causing her to drop to her knees. Now that was it; they had to leave! I witnessed this crazy man reaching inside my screen door, grabbing this girl from her seat and slapping her to the floor. Oh yeah, they had to go. I shouted that they had to leave and without hesitation, they all left. This picture was so familiar to me, and that is why I couldn't allow that in my house or in my life anymore.

The next day, I received a call from Jarvis with a disturbing tone in his voice. I just had to know what happened after they left my house. I thought that their evening would be over. I thought wrong.

I asked him, "What was wrong with your boy last night and what happened after you guys left my house?"

He suggested that I sit down before he started his story. "First off," he started, "after all that mess that we went through at your house earlier that day, we ended up dropping Katrina's baby at her mother's house and made our way to a hotel room. Everything was cool in the beginning. Angie and I had our room and Rudy and Katrina had their room; we were enjoying ourselves for a few hours. Later that evening, we all got together in one room that Rudy was in and everything was going great. I don't really know what happened but after we had a little alcohol to drink, Rudy and Katrina began to argue and fight again."

Now he had my attention because I just knew that something went on that would tip the meter over. He continued the story. "They began to kick and fight with each other like they really hated each other. Angie and I couldn't take any more of this mess, so we broke the fight up before the front office started calling us asking questions. He picked Angie up like he was going to hug her to apologize to her but it seemed for a split second that he freaked out. Just like a pit bull, he attacked her like he was a professional wrestler. He clotheslined her over the bed that was in the room. Man, I thought that I was watching the WWE after he pulled that stunt."

We both were silent for a split second. I mentioned to him that men like that are going to be locked up in a prison cell, thinking that they can hit on women like that. Now that was all of the proof that I needed to stay away from Rudy and then to try to cope with how people can live with themselves fighting in a relationship. After listening to the story, I knew that I was glad to be out of the relationship that I had been involved in.

Once Again

I'VE LEARNED FROM ALL MY YEARS OF SCHOOL THAT HISTORY TENDS to repeat itself. There was an emptiness in my life that I needed to fill. I guess in a strange way, I was bored. I needed something that was high energy in my life. I wanted the type of energy or excitement that was involved in my last relationship with Joy and if it wasn't on that level, then I wasn't going to be satisfied.

I needed to see Joy and I really missed her. She was the only excitement that I knew so I was desperate to see her. I hadn't seen her for a few months, so I thought that time would heal a broken heart and a wounded relationship. I made the call to see if she missed me and if she wanted to spend some time with me. Once again, we began to see each other and became more intimate, as if we really wanted each other. We continued to see each other and spend time with each other. There was nothing exclusive about our relationship. We would see each other on occasions and talk to each other occasionally. As I recall, the relationship was set up so that during the week we would talk and then Friday and Saturday we were together.

I was seeing other women while Joy and I were away from each other. I just liked the attention that I was receiving. Although I was seeing Joy and the other female friends that I was involved with, there was still an emptiness. I wanted a change in my life. I even considered cutting everybody else off and planned on a long life with Joy. In a strange way, I thought that we were meant to be together. I had heard the stories that couples beat the pulp out of each other, marry and then somehow work things out. I had the idea to attempt this feat. I was planning on surprising her by buying her an engagement ring and telling her that I wanted to marry her. I wanted her and her son to be in my life forever.

Just when I got up enough courage to ask her hand in marriage, I received some wise counsel. I ended up talking to a friend of mine I hadn't seen in years. My friend, Demetrius was as funny as I was. He was someone that had either been there or knew of someone that had been through it. One thing for certain was that he had an answer for everything.

I remember the magic words that started my thought process. "Are you crazy?" he asked. "Boy, you know that nothing good comes from an abusive relationship. Nothing but being stiff in the pants and heartbroken."

Wow, it'd been a long time since anyone had spoken so open and bluntly with me. I really had to take heed and listen to wisdom. One thing that he advised I do was remember what my dad would say: to run and run fast. His advice was to get away and stay away before one of us killed the other or one of us ended up in jail for the rest of our lives. I took his advice and I had to devise a plan to permanently get her out of my system, this time for good.

I remember one time sitting in my living room just replaying the last couple of years in my mind. I had a vision of my mother come to me. My mother and I were having this wonderful conversation and suddenly she asked me, "So, did you get that crazy devil child out of your hair yet? Well, if you didn't, you must like it! Go ahead and keep on fighting and getting beat up by a girl. Go ahead and get locked up again. Go ahead and keep on wasting your time and energy on a girl that doesn't want you."

The next thing that my mother said had me thinking and just tore me apart. She said that if I kept that charade up, it was probably going to send her to an early grave. Now that was all the fuel that I needed to begin to make a change in my life.

The Final Straw

THE TIME WAS NOW! I HAD DECIDED TO GIVE UP ON THIS DESTRUCTIVE and abusive relationship. I couldn't seem to get anything accomplished while I was dealing with this anger issue. I had to rid myself of the complete ignorance and disrespect that Joy showed toward me.

We were at the point in our relationship that even her son didn't want to be around me anymore. Truthfully, I understood because I wouldn't want to deal with any man continuing to hit, yell at, curse at and abuse my mother. I was beginning to wrestle with so many things in my mind at this point. I honestly wanted to just crawl under a rock and die. I was thinking that being locked up was better for me than being a free man. I knew that it was time to make a drastic change once I started having these unusual thoughts.

I was sinking into a state of depression. Depression is defined as a state of feeling sadness or dejection. It is a disorder that is characterized by a difficulty in reasoning and a sense of hopelessness. Through all this stuff, I really hadn't had a big appetite and I wasn't well at all.

I began to see less and less of her. Truthfully, although I could not stand the sight of her, I missed her body. Every single time that I was tempted to call her, I reminded myself of all the arguing, the fussing and all of the fistfights. After all that stuff that I went through, every urge went away. I had a desire more than ever to be free from Joy.

It had been three weeks and I hadn't heard from Joy. Yes, what a relief! I was getting confident enough to begin and meeting new women. Although I was free, I still wanted a serious relationship. Maybe the right lady would make me forget about Joy and take her completely out of my system.

Just like clockwork, an entire month had passed by and guess who decided to show up? Yup, you guessed it: the she-devil herself, Joy.

"After all of this time, you have the nerve to just show up?" I asked. "Are you crazy? I'm really over you and I just want you to leave me alone!"

I had never seen her like this. There were real tears in her eyes. I just watched her as she hung her head down and walked slowly to her car. This was new to see—no fuss; she just walked away. As she got into her car, I watched her just sitting there with her head down on the steering wheel. *Hmmm, maybe I finally got through to her. Maybe she has finally taken me seriously.* Sadly enough, I just couldn't let her sit out there crying.

I walked off of my porch and tapped on her window for her to let me in to talk to her. "Is it really over for good? Do you have another woman in the house?" she asked.

Why were there so many questions when I was trying to break up? I assured her that I was going to attempt to get my life back on track. If I had to be away from her, then so be it! She began to cry harder than ever before. Since she had the car running, I shut the ignition switch off and asked her to come into the house and calm down. I didn't think that it was safe for her to drive in that condition. As you probably can guess, it wasn't really a struggle to get her out of the car.

At this point, I only had one thing on my mind. My goal was to have sex with her one more time and then that was totally it; she had to go! I gave her a consoling kiss on the lips and then she said, "I thought that it was over. I thought that you were breaking up with me. You're kissing me all in my mouth and now I guess that you want sex? Well, just come on and get it over with!"

I looked her in her eyes and walked over to her as if I wanted to grab her—well, I did. I lifted her up over my shoulder and carried her into my bedroom. I was going to give her what we wanted. No, we weren't going to make love; we were going to have uncensored, "I really miss you", "I'm sorry" sex! This was going to be the kind of sex that we were going to ask God for forgiveness for. As I said all the while, our sex life wasn't the issue; it was when we were done that we had problems.

After we both got out of the shower and were done putting the bedroom back in place, she had to leave to take care of some errands for her mother. She asked me to come to her mother's house around six o'clock that evening and sit with her. Man, after what we had just finished doing, I would have met her on the moon if she had asked me. I had more chores around the house to finish and then I was taking a nap, and that was exactly what I did.

Not Again

WHEN I CAME UPSTAIRS AT JOY'S, I NOTICED ONE OF THE COUSIN'S daughters was having a wonderful conversation with someone on the other end of the phone. After I grabbed the phone from her, I was met with a dial tone on the other end. I was watching the kids jumping around, playing a game and having a really great time. After thirty minutes had passed, I suggested that they should take a break from the game because the girls wanted to watch a movie.

As we were all starting to nod off, there was a thunderous knock at the front door. When Joy's mother answered the door, it was the city police stating that they were doing a follow-up on a phone call. The only thing that I kept hearing was that no one called the police, and no one was in trouble. The officers asked if they could search around the house because a child called the 911 line and by law, they had to investigate anything that involved children.

I went into a panic state because I assumed that the visit from the officers was to escort me straight to jail. Could this feeling that I had all day long be warning me that this could have been the visit to do me in? Any one of her family members could have reported me to the police. The person who could have sealed the deal for me spending years in jail would have been her son. I imagined them interrogating him, and he wouldn't have any choice but to tell the truth about what he had seen. Most of what he ever witnessed was a lot of screaming, continuous fighting and fussing. I knew that if I wasn't careful, this relationship was going to land me in jail for a very long time or be what would cause my death. Panic was seizing my mind. I felt like I was being set up, listening to Joy's mother insist that the officers had no reason or no right to come into their house.

She became very abrupt with the officers, yelling, "No one from this house called the police."

Since the kids were upstairs with me, they yelled my name…It sounded like a set-up. Suddenly, I heard the sounds of the jail-house doors slamming shut in my head, *CLANG!* Trying to make sense of everything, I rushed downstairs with nothing but anxiety, repeating to myself, *This is a set-up; you're going down.* As I entered the room that was full of Joy's family and the city's finest in blue, something in me was unsettled. The police continued to insist that some child called, and they needed to make sure no one was in danger, or no child was being hurt. Now, with all eyes on me, the officers asked, "Sir, do you know if any child has called the police department?"

As calmly as I could, I told them about the young girl who was having a conversation with someone on the phone, but when I took the phone from her to see who she was talking to, I only heard a dial tone. I felt the room closing in as I stood there between the officers and her family members. With fear gripping my heart, I felt that this could go wrong very quickly.

Secure that the scene was deemed safe, the officers left without any further questions. Something in me wanted to run and escape as far as I could from this location. I walked back up the stairs, while listening to her family laughing and joking that the police never show up when you really need them. That walk back up the stairs seemed like a walk of death. Step by step, my mind kept saying *RUN—GET OUT NOW!* I heard my father's voice, "Son, warning always comes before destruction." Was this God's way of getting my attention? Was this God's way of arresting me? This relationship, this situation, was too much and had become very uncomfortable for me. I needed an exit plan! *I hear you, God! It is time to make my exodus happen. I cannot take this anymore. I need to get out, but how?*

Not So Clean Severing

SLOWLY BUT SURELY, I STARTED SPEAKING TO AND SEEING JOY LESS. I no longer wanted to be around her or associate with anyone who was connected to her. I continued to ask myself, *Why am I staying?* I was certain that I wanted her out of my life, and I was determined to make this happen. Realizing that it was the physical connection keeping me bonded to her, I stopped coming around completely. If I didn't make a move, one of us was going to truly get hurt. Something in me was finished.

After a month, I began to entertain the idea of meeting other people. I was not sure what Joy was doing; I didn't care. Someone else could have the headache of dealing with Joy. This woman was the opposite of her name; she was pure evil, and no one would ever be safe with her in their life.

Even though I was no longer around her and she was now becoming a distant memory, I still wanted female companionship. I wasn't necessarily looking to replace Joy; I just wanted a new start and a new relationship. I was looking to find someone who could love me, and that's when Jasmine came into my life. Could this be the change that I was looking for? Was this my new beginning? I really liked her and wanted to get to know her better. Not only were we hanging out and dating, I wanted to introduce her to my family. My brother called and told me that he was cooking and that he wanted me to come out so he could meet my new girlfriend.

As we were having a great time at my brother's house, my cell phone rang. Staring at my phone, I saw Joy's number. I felt perplexed but compelled to answer. "Hello?" I sighed with relief; it was Joy's son.

"Dad," he said, "what are you doing?" Not really knowing what to say, I simply told him that I was hanging out with some friends and was not home. He then wanted to know when I was coming to pick him up and hang out with him. Tears formed in my eyes. I not only had a connection with his mother, but I really looked at this little one like he was mine. With everything in me, I replied, "Son, this is going to be the last time that I can talk to you. Your mom and I are not together anymore, and I will not be coming around any longer." I explained to him that I would always care about him, but it was time for me to move on.

I was unsure what he told his mother, but my cell phone rang repeatedly with her obviously looking for answers. I never answered her calls and I refused to entertain her nonsense now. Since we hadn't spoken in a while, I didn't want to have that torment anymore. I made the mistake of checking the ten messages that were left on my voicemail.

Noticeably upset, my brother was staring at me, asking me, "What is wrong?"

Although I tried to hide this moment from Jasmine, she noticed something was wrong. Once again, I was faced with feelings of being trapped in something I was no longer a part of. I was livid and wanted to rip someone's head off. As I pressed to hear the last message, the voice that I despised so much stated that she was coming to my house to kill me. What was really going on? I had not spoken to her in months, I had moved on with my life...and now this? Caught in this triangle, I felt so bad, because it seemed that I was involving Jasmine in this war with Joy. No longer enjoying myself, I cut the visit with my brother short. In my head, I was now preparing myself just in case this looney tune really decided to come to my house.

We had been back at my house for about forty-five minutes when my cell phone began ringing and there was an aggressive knock on my front door. I was not expecting company and I was curious to know who it was. As I headed toward the door, I glanced down and I realized that Joy was calling. What did she want? Who was at my front door? My phone would not stop ringing and whoever was at my door would not stop knocking.

For some reason, I could not see who was on the other side of the door. I cautiously latched the security bolt and proceeded to open the door. When I slightly opened the door, Joy was forcibly trying to open the door to get inside. At a glance, I noticed that she had three other girls with her. These hood rats were fueled by rage that was spearheaded by this woman seeking revenge. When they could not get into the house, they began to destroy my property outside. I could hear the rocks being hurled at my truck windows. I heard the smashing sounds of something hitting my vehicle. Looking outside, I could see everything that was in their line of sight was being ransacked and destroyed.

Instead of trying to take on this band of vigilantes, I decided to protect myself and everything that was inside my house. I decided to call the police to get them to intervene. After ten minutes of destruction, the police still had not arrived. After all the cursing, crashing and destruction, I saw that this crazed lunatic had gone mad and smashed out every window in my truck. Every single window, mirrors, and doors had been smashed in by these four crazy ladies. My clean, polished waxed truck now looked like it had been in some type of war zone. What in the world was going on?

I called the 911 operator again, and they just repeated that officers were on their way. It had been over twenty-five minutes and I was ready to take matters into my own hands. I grabbed my baseball bat and started walking toward the door. Jasmine grabbed my arm and begged me not to go outside until the police came.

"I'm going to kill you!" Joy's voice taunted. "I dare you to come outside and fight me now."

She continued to hurl threats and throw things at my house. At this point, I'd had it. I pushed past Jasmine, knocking her to the ground, not trying to hurt her, but not allowing any one to stand in my way. I charged outside to fight everyone and anything in my sight. With the baseball bat in my hand, and the voice of God trying to reason with me, I was now at the point of no return. I did not care; I wanted to hurt her! As they saw me charging toward them, they all jumped into their car and drove away. But instead of leaving, they circled the block, riding around as if they were doing a verbal drive-by. I felt like the devil himself was taunting me to no end.

"You will never be able to get away from me; you will always be trapped; this is your life," she said.

I was called everything under the sun. I was cursed at by all four of these heathens. Looking like a lost dog with no control, I chased them up the road, trying to outrun and jump on the car to get my hands on them.

After forty-five minutes, the police showed up from one direction as Joy's car was going in the opposite direction. When the lead officer came to me, I pointed, showing him Joy's car.

"Officer!" I yelled. "That's the car that she is driving in. The girls in that car destroyed my property and busted my truck. Can you go after her? I want to press charges."

The officer said that since she was gone, there was nothing they were going to do. They suggested that I file for a restraining order and that would cause her to stay away from me once she was served. I was so upset that these officers did nothing to go after her but looked at me as if I was the weak one. Once again, I was in a situation where nothing was being done and she seemed justified. It was unfair that she just got away with the destruction of my property.

The next day, I followed the officer's instructions and went to the county courthouse to file for a restraining order. What was interesting about this trip was it seemed like everyone at the front desk thought that I was telling the funniest joke. I heard small snickers of disbelief that I, a man, was filing for a restraining order. I was serious and committed to ridding my life of Joy. Through this process, I felt embarrassed and angry because I was filing paperwork to keep a woman from me.

I assumed that Joy received the restraining order. Two weeks later, I received a recorded phone message that I was a coward, and other creative words that she could come up with to state how upset she was. In the message, she promised that I would not see the last of her and this restraining order would not stop her.

When I had enough of the harassing phone calls, as bold as I could be, I told her that I would blow the entire house up that she and her family lived in. "If you come around me or my house ever again, I promise you, I am going to remind you of everything that you and your girls destroyed," I shouted.

Was this the end of this reckless relationship? Like a calm early morning, I heard my mother's voice: "Son, let it go." That was it; it was over. I was finished!

Jasmine and I were no longer together. She told me that she did not sign up for that type of drama and did not want that kind of fight in her life. Although she didn't want to be in a relationship with me, I was at peace. I felt like someone untied my straps and released me from years of bondage. I was free!

True Confession
and Closure

THERE NEEDS TO BE A FLAG WAVED TOWARD DATING ABUSE AND abusive relationships. People allow their emotions to rule over them instead of evaluating and rationalizing the entire situation. An alarming number of young men and women are in correctional institutions because of abuse and the result of an abusive relationship.

I was in one of those relationships and I knew that I needed to make changes in my own life. I had to identify my anger issues and I had to find a way to deal with being angry and abusive. I allowed my anger to control my decision making and I lost control of rational thinking. I reacted when I felt that my manhood was being challenged.

I thought that a physical relationship cemented a relationship. I thought that sex was the best and only way to show attraction. Although sex is a wonderful tool, it should be shared between two people who share a common love for each other. It should be practiced between couples who can be committed to each other and no one else. Sex between the couple should not only enhance but accompany the relationship.

What is the issue? People these days use their anatomy for manipulation. This act is defined as influencing and managing shrewdly or deviously. This also means to tamper with or falsify for personal gain. At no time should anyone use their body to masterfully slow walk and turn anyone out. Some people try to make you feel as if no one can please you sexually quite like them. Honestly, there will always be more skillful lovers that will make you forget about the person that is abusing and saying that they are by far the best thing that you had ever experienced.

What is physical abuse? Physical abuse is a method of abuse used by people to physically harm or hurt a person by punching, kicking and fighting with an individual. Most abusive people believe that fighting with people proves that you are the better person. How absurd! There are men that believe, as I did, that hitting on women makes you feel like a man. There are some poor, delusional women that believe that a man loves them more when he is fighting and yelling at them. This is never a way to show how much you love someone.

Early detection is the key to identify an aggressive and abusive person. Generally, small signs begin to show, such as small pushing, aggressive bumping, smacking on any parts of the body. Most of the times, this will lead to punching, kicking and excessive fighting.

No one should ever live their lives like this. No one should ever have to suffer from any kind of abuse. Whether it is mental, verbal, physical, sexual or any other type of abuse, it is not a safe environment for individuals to be involved in.

This message is directed to the inexperienced dater: Do not ever lose control of yourselves and never step out of the character that

God has created you to be.

There are some people that want to be the dominant factor in a relationship. The stubborn, control-hungry individuals in relationships generally demand things be done their way. Nothing else seems to matter or nothing will be done unless it is done that person's way. Some people thrive off controlling and preying upon others. They seem to think that making another person fear them proves dominance. Unless these issues are realized and discussed, a destructive generation of abusers will continue to destroy emotions, goals and dreams.

My Straight Jacket is simply described as self-bondage. Sometimes we allow ourselves to be bound or tied up in a relationship. Abuse binds people like a white straight jacket as if to keep arms and hands restrained. A straitjacket is a garment shaped like a jacket with overlong sleeves and is typically used to restrain a person who may otherwise cause harm to him/herself or others. Once the arms are inserted into the straitjacket's sleeves, they are then crossed across the chest. The ends of the sleeves are then tied to the back of the wearer, ensuring that the arms are kept close to the chest with as little movement as possible. The jacket prevents the sufferer from injuring himself or others around, from damaging clothes or furniture, and from injuring staff or fellow inmates.

A word of warning: Someone under a lot of stress and pressure will find the fastest way to release their frustration. Most of the time, circumstances will have escalated because of the reactions to physical, sexual and verbal abuse. When this occurs, you are a victim of your own personal prison. I saw a profound statement a few years ago: An idle mind is the devil's workshop. The mind has time to imagine and wander, especially when it is lying dormant. It is wise to maintain a healthy and active lifestyle and not allow the mind to race with emotions.

In conclusion, be aware of your family history. Some abusers are a product of how they are raised. It is a sad statement, but abuse is a learned behavior. Some people believe that they are going to run their relationship just like their parents did. A lot of times, we witness members of our family actively fighting and being abusive.

There should be more communication in relationships. People should avoid, as much as possible, confrontations in front of children. A key thing to remember is that children are natural copiers. They repeat actions and say the things that they hear. Children start their lives innocently, and then life becomes a dress rehearsal. When being influenced by parents, family members, the Internet, and social media, children have all sorts of bad influences with domestic violence. Even basic television shows continual arguing and fighting between partners. We need to take an aggressive effort to prevent abuse. Whatever the person, whatever the source, whomever the victim, this dangerous trend has to stop.

I pray that this book encouraged someone to remove the blinders from their eyes, especially if they are involved in an abusive relationship. People should take time to really get to know the person they want to be in a relationship with. Your life is not worth losing for the act of being violent. Remember, you do not have to live in a situation where you are being abused or are abusing people. A life change should be considered when you resort to fighting to release anger. No one will ever win in an abusive relationship—no one!